EDGE BOOKS™

GROSS

GROSS BRAIN TEASERS

GUIDES

by Marne Ventura

CAPSTONE PRESS
a capstone imprint

Edge Books are published by Capstone Press,
1710 Roe Crest Drive, North Mankato, Minnesota 56003
www.capstonepub.com

Library of Congress Cataloging-in-Publication Data
Ventura, Marne.
Gross brain teasers / by Marne Ventura.
p. cm.—(Edge books: gross guides)
Summary: "Lists fun brain teasers with a fun, gross theme"—Provided
by publisher.
Includes bibliographical references and index.
ISBN 978-1-4296-9923-5 (library binding)
ISBN 978-1-4765-1382-9 (ebook pdf)
1. Puzzles—Juvenile literature. 2. Logic puzzles—Juvenile literature. 3. Lateral
thinking puzzles—Juvenile literature. I. Title.
GV1493.V46 2013
793.73—dc23   2012030971

Editorial Credits
Mandy Robbins, editor; Tracy McCabe, designer; Marcie Spence, media researcher;
Laura Manthe, production specialist

Photo Credits
Alamy Images: Rick & Nora Bowers, 17; Capstone Studio: Karon Dubke, design
element, 16 (bottom right); Dreamstime: Snezana, 16 (bottom left); iStockphoto:
Damian Evans 16 (top); Shutterstock: anaken2012, cover (calculator), Andrey
Armyagov, 20 (bottom), Anton Gvozdikov, 10, Christphe Testi, 19, Christos
Georghiou, cover (design element), Danny Smythe, 26, design56, 14 (middle),
Dja65, 22, Eric Isselee, 25 (top), Fedorov Oleksiy, design element, 6, hellea, 20 (top),
Holly Kuchera, 11 (bottom), Julia Ivantsova, cover (pencil), Konstantin Sutyagin,
20 (middle), Kuttelvaserova, 21, Leigh Prather, cover (design element), Mariyana
Misaleva, 12, margita, 12-13, Mircea Bezergheanu, 24 (right), Petr Vaclavek, cover
(design element), Piotr Marcinski, cover (woman), 4 (woman), Pling, cover (design
element), rodho, (top), S. Matveev, 27, Sebastian Kaulitzki, 5 (front), 8, 9, Sergy
Goruppa, 23 (front), 25 (bottom), Sergey Kamshylin, 23 (back), sergign, 7, spaxiax, 11
(top right), SunnyS, 11 (top left), Vector Ninja, cover (brain), 4, (brain), XAOC, cover
(design element), xpixel, 24 (left)

Printed in the United States of America in Brainerd, Minnesota.
092012   006938BANGS13

Table of Contents

Let's Get Gross!

When it comes to brainpower, you have to exercise your mental muscle in order to stay sharp. But why strain your brain with dull word problems and puzzles? Sharpen your skills while learning facts disgusting enough to gag a maggot.

For starters, brush up on your gross vocabulary. Unscramble these words to find different ways to say "gross." The first one is done for you.

leiv = vile

gisgidsutn

kcyyu

louf

esuprelvi

nltrvoige

cgsiiennk

ciyk

GROSS ORGANISMS ON YOUR SKIN

You are not alone—ever. Microscopic animals called demodex mites live on your face at all times. They burrow into your eyelash follicles. These mites eat your dead skin cells and lay eggs on you.

George and Henry look at their skin scrapings under a microscope. George finds five mites every day for six days. Henry finds eight mites every day for four days. "You have more mites than I do," says George. "No, we have the same," jokes Henry, "because 5 x 6 = 8 x 4." What is Henry's joke?

FACT

It takes about 100 demodex mites placed end to end to measure 1 inch (2.5 centimeters).

Without moving it, change the position of the middle mite so it's not in the middle.

microscopic—too small to be seen without a microscope
follicle—a small sac or cavity in the body, such as for hair

The average human is covered with 2 square yards (1.8 square meters) of skin. Guess how many **bacteria** live there? As many as there are people in the United States—that's roughly 300 million.

If you're covered with 2 square yards (1.8 sq m) of skin, how many square feet of skin do you have?
(Hint: 1 square yard = 3 x 3 feet)

If your skin is covered evenly with bacteria, about how many live on 1 square foot (30.5 square centimeters)?

Have you ever wondered how many bacteria live in your armpit? Take the number of bacteria on 1 square foot (30.5 sq cm) of skin from the last question. Multiply it by three, because your armpit is three times more germy. Now divide it by four, since your armpit is about 0.25 square foot (8 sq cm).

Use this equation: (16,666,666 x 3)/4=

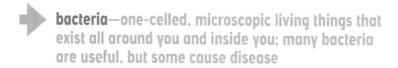

bacteria—one-celled, microscopic living things that exist all around you and inside you; many bacteria are useful, but some cause disease

Mrs. Mud tells her son Dusty to get a clean hand towel for each of her children. Dusty has as many sisters as brothers, but each sister has only half as many sisters as brothers.

How many towels does Dusty need?

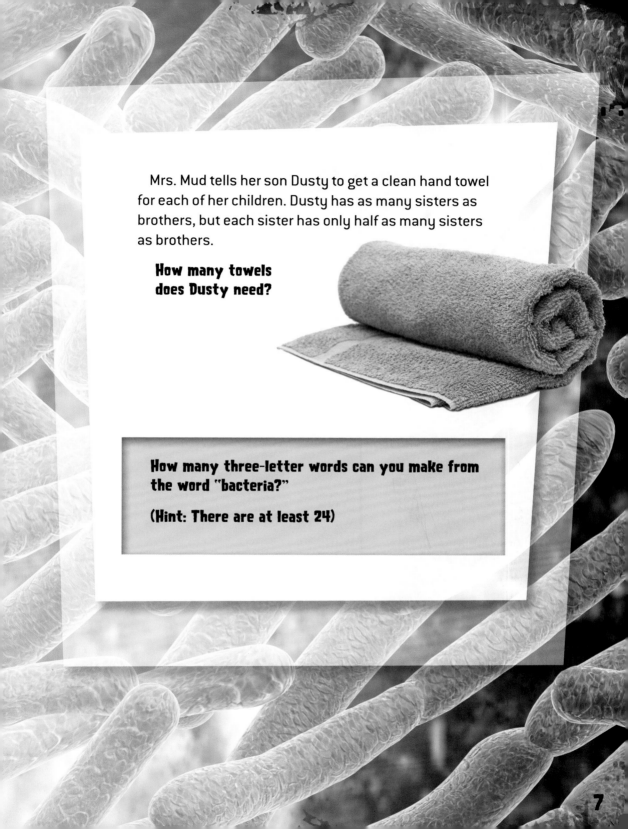

How many three-letter words can you make from the word "bacteria?"

(Hint: There are at least 24)

GROSS ORGANISMS IN YOUR HOME

Hundreds of thousands of dust mites live in your home. What do they do there? They eat your dead skin cells and poop on your belongings. People who sneeze, wheeze, and itch in a dusty room are not allergic to dust. Dust mite poop is the culprit.

Spell the word that answers each clue below. One or two vowels are done for you. You fill in the missing letters.

Instrument needed to see a dust mite: __ I __ __ __ __ __ O __ __

Blood-sucking animal related to the dust mite: __ I __ __

What you do when you're allergic to dust mite poop: __ __ E __ __ E

Web-spinning animal related to the dust mite: __ __ I __ __ __

What dust mites do on your stuff: __ __ O __

How many legs a dust mite has: E __ __ __ __

Change DUST to MITE, one letter at a time, in four tries. Each time you change a letter, you should still be spelling a real word. There is more than one way to do it. Use the following example changing "NOSE" to "MOSS" to get you started:

NOSE

1. HOSE

2. HOST

3. MOST

4. MOSS

Dust mite poop is covered with a peritrophic membrane. Certain proteins in this poop "skin" are what cause most dust mite allergies. An average dust mite poops about 20 times a day. The poop is so tiny that it floats invisibly in the air, and it is easily inhaled by humans.

"Poop" is a palindrome. That means it is spelled the same forward and backward. Can you name these palindromes?

Nickname for mother:
Nickname for father:
Canoe first used by Eskimos:
A word for fart:
Lunchtime:

The words below have been separated into pairs of letters by hungry dust mites. Put the letter pairs back in order to spell five places where dust mites live. The first one is done for you.

1. Something goes in it. Your head goes on it:
ow se pi ca ll = pillowcase

2. When you sleep, it springs into action to support you:
tt ma ss re

3. It has arms and legs, but no face, and you sit on it:
mc ar ir ha

4. You would be too cool if you slept without these:
an bl ts ke

5. The neighbors are glad you have these when you change clothes:
rt cu ns ai

 allergic—when something that is not harmful to most people makes someone feel sick; many allergies make you sneeze

You've probably heard of the "five-second rule," right? If you drop your food, it's safe to eat if you pick it up in 5 seconds. This is a rule that is meant to be broken. Researchers say bacteria is transferred almost instantly.

Unlock the code to decipher the message. For each letter, write the letter that comes before it in the alphabet.

Epo'u fbu gppe uibu't cffo po uif gmpps.

James and Jennifer have a watermelon seed spitting contest. A seed that sticks to the ceiling is worth five points. A seed that sticks to the wall scores four points. A seed that sticks to the refrigerator earns three points. Who wins, and by how many points?

	James	Jennifer
Ceiling	5	4
Wall	4	6
Refrigerator	7	9

Mom is mad. For each point they scored, James and Jennifer have to do two minutes of cleanup. How many hours and minutes do they each work?

decipher—to figure out something that is written in code or is hard to understand

James drops his peanut butter and pickle sandwich on his dog Grungy on the second day of June. Nine days later, Grungy rolls in the grass. Three days before Grungy rolls in the grass, James drops a tuna and potato chip sandwich on Grungy. Six days after the tuna sandwich incident, Grungy plays in a mud puddle. Two days before Grungy frolics in the mud, James comes down with the stomach flu.

On what day of the month does James get sick?

Poor James. On the first day he throws up twice as many times as he does on the second day.

If his total number of pukes is 12, how many barfs does he do on the first day, and how many on the second?

GROSS BODY FACTS

Snot, phlegm, boogers—whatever you call it, mucus keeps you healthy. It prevents your nasal tissues from drying out and traps bacteria and dust before they enter your body. Mucus is 95 percent water, so drinking water helps your mucus do its job.

Olivia decided to double her water intake every day. On the first day she drank 8 ounces (237 milliliters) of water. On which day did Olivia drink 64 ounces (1,893 mL) of water?

Your body produces all kinds of fluids. Some are slimy, some are smelly, and all are gross. Unscramble the words below for a list of favorites.

olbdo   mvito   vlsaia
nueir   umucs   ups
aswte

phlegm—the thick snot that is produced when someone has a cold
tissue—a layer or bunch of soft material that makes up body parts

My first letter is in **GUTS** and **SNOT** but not in **FART**.

My second letter is in **SCAT** and **CLOT** but not in **STOOL**.

My third letter is in **SALIVA** and **TEARS** but not in **SLIME**.

My fourth letter is in **SLOBBER** and **BOOGER** but not in **GROSS**.

What am I?

Find the body fluid in each sentence.
The first one is done for you.

I gues**s we at**e the whole cake.

He's got ears on the sides of his head.

They found fur in every den.

Bravo, Mitchell!

Professor Putrid labeled his body fluid samples, but the labels came unglued during the night. The professor keeps his samples on two shelves that each hold three containers. **Use the clues to put the labels back where they belong.**

BLOOD	TEARS	EARWAX
MUCUS	SALIVA	SWEAT

Clue #1: BLOOD is below MUCUS, left of TEARS, and right of SALIVA.

Clue #2: EARWAX is above SALIVA.

HAZARDOUS WASTE

BLOOD   MUCUS   TEARS   SALIVA   EARWAX   SWEAT

Do you know why it's important to stay hydrated? Because you're mostly water!

Total Body:	60% water
Brain:	70% water
Lungs:	90% water
Lean Muscle:	75% water
Body Fat:	10% water
Bones:	22% water
Blood:	83% water

Which letter of the alphabet answers each clue?

Clue: urine
Clue: body part you use for vision
Clue: what you do with your eyes

Change a letter in each word to name a gross body part or fluid. The first one is done for you.

pea = pee	snow	pure
faces	mutt	lives
note		

GROSS ANIMALS

Male capuchin monkeys pee into their hands and then rub the urine into their fur. Scientists believe these monkeys do this to let females know they are ready to mate.

Scientist Sabrina needs to take a python, a monkey, and a bunch of bananas across the river to her research lab. Her boat is only big enough for herself and one other thing. If left alone, the monkey will eat the bananas and the python will swallow the monkey.

How does she get them all safely across the river? (Hint: There are two possible solutions.)

Instead of dropping their waste, skipper caterpillars fire their poop like a cannonball. The pellets travel as much as 40 times the length of the caterpillars' bodies. Scientists think the caterpillars are trying to fool predators who find their next meal by following the smell of caterpillar feces.

As lonely Dave walked to the zoo,

He spied six caterpillars firing poo.

Each caterpillar shot six poos,

Each poo hit someone's shoe.

Each shoe was one of two.

Caterpillars, poos, and shoes,

How many people going to the zoo?

predator—an animal that hunts other animals for food
feces—the semi-solid waste that people and animals pass out of their bodies

Scientist Sabrina and Professor Putrid are walking through the rainforest when they see four caterpillars sitting on a leaf. "I'll bet you can't tell me when three 3's equal 4," says Sabrina. "Yes, I can," answers the Professor.

What is his answer?
(Hint: The professor writes an equation.)

Giraffes seem like tall, graceful animals, but one of a giraffe's body parts is gag-inducing. A giraffe's tongue is 18 inches (46 cm) long and is dripping with thick, slimy saliva. This saliva helps the giraffe eat and **digest** dry leaves from treetops. Giraffes also use their tongues to clean out their noses. Just imagine picking your nose with your tongue!

digest—to break down food so it can be used by the body

Slurpy the giraffe loves Zoey the zookeeper and follows her everywhere. After Zoey ties Slurpy to a tree, the zookeeper's cart rolls away and ends up near the tree. How can Zoey get her cart back without getting slimed by Slurpy?

Can you think of at least five different words for drool?

FACT

To help produce so much slime, a giraffe consumes up to 12 gallons (45 liters) of water a day.

Flies are so annoying. They buzz around your picnic lunch and land on your lemonade. Next time you wave your hand to chase away a fly, think about this. Flies eat poop and are covered with all kinds of nasty bacteria. While sitting on your sandwich they vomit enzymes to digest it. Then they suck it through their tube-shaped tongue.

For a science project, Sam and Sofia recorded the number of flies that landed on a trash can. Here is what they each wrote on a blank sheet of paper:

$$1 + 9 + 1 + 9 + 1$$

The next day, they added up the number of flies. Sam got 21, but Sofia got 15. **What happened?**

Use the code to fill in the names of diseases spread by flies.

2-7-13-10-4-15-1 = C H O L E R A
11-1-10-1-15-8-1 =
20-4-10-10-13-19   5-4-18-4-15 =
16-10-4-4-14-8-12-6   16-8-2-9-12-4-16-16 =
3-20-16-4-12-17-4-15-20 =

A=1	G=6	M=11	S=16
C=2	H=7	N=12	T=17
D=3	I=8	O=13	V=18
E=4	K=9	P=14	W=19
F=5	L=10	R=15	Y=20

Sofia and Sam are walking on the beach. They discover a pile of seaweed that's swarming with flies. Sofia counts 27 flies on a single leaf. Sam counts twice as many flies on one seaweed bulb.

If you combined Sam and Sofia's flies, how many would you have? What equation would you use to solve this problem?
(There is more than one answer.)

If you lined the flies up side-by-side, what would the total width be?
Hint: An adult fly with its wings out measures about 0.5 inch (1.27 cm) across.

And if you lined the flies up end to end, what would the total length be?
Hint: An adult fly with its wings out measures 0.25 inch (0.64 cm) long.

Use the clues to unscramble the words.

Flies are covered with this: C A A E I R T B
Flies eat this for dinner: E E S C F
Flies spread this: D S S E E A I
Flies vomit these: Z M S N E Y E

GROSS HISTORY

Have you ever thought about where people peed and pooped before the invention of the toilet? From ancient times until about 100 years ago, many people used bowls called chamber pots to hold their waste. They kept them under their beds at night.

In exactly three moves, turn over these three chamber pots two at a time. You want to end up with all the chamber pots upside down. Every chamber pot must be turned over at least once. There is more than one way to do it.

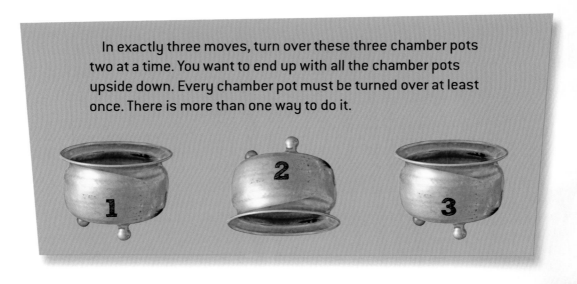

Change FART to POOP by changing one letter at a time. Make sure you're spelling a real word each time you change a letter.

FART _____ _____ _____ _____ POOP

During World War I (1914–1918), wounded soldiers who didn't get immediate treatment often died. Doctors noticed that men who survived had maggots in their wounds. Scientists later discovered that maggots eat away dead tissue and bacteria that can cause infection.

Five maggots are in a dish. How do you divide them among five wounded soldiers so that each soldier gets a maggot, but one maggot remains in the dish?

Doctors still use maggots to clean wounds today. This practice is called maggot therapy. Unscramble the letters below to spell seven words related to maggot therapy and its history.

isledro	aaceirbt	nretttmea
ownddeu	setius	cosrtdo
tinoeinfc		

infection—an illness caused by germs such as bacteria or viruses

In the early 1800s, doctors believed that illnesses were caused by too much blood in one part of the body. They put slimy worms called leeches on the diseased body part. Each leech would use a sucker on its front end to latch on and drain blood from the human.

How can you arrange 16 leeches in 10 lines of four leeches each?

Use the letters in LEECHES and BLOOD to answer these clues:

S __ __ __ __   I was once someone's home but can be found on the beach.

D __ __ __   I'm a child's playmate, but I never grow up.

B __ __ __ __   Sometimes I look blue and sometimes red, but you need me inside you to not be dead.

B __ __ __ __   I'm quiet inside your body, but loud when I come out.

S __ __ __   I'm lazy and messy. I'm not a blob or a glob, but a...?

Professor Putrid has eight maggots. Their names are:

Kooky   Slimy   Tickler   Bloody

Slick   Muncher   Jumpy   Ugly

**He keeps them in a special case in alphabetical order.
Arrange them for Professor Putrid.**

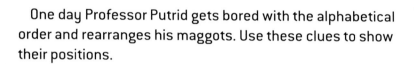

One day Professor Putrid gets bored with the alphabetical order and rearranges his maggots. Use these clues to show their positions.

Muncher is to the right of Slimy.

Slick is to the left of Kooky and to the right of Muncher.

Bloody is underneath Muncher.

Ugly is to the left of Bloody.

Jumpy is underneath Kooky.

GROSS FOOD

Because it's so difficult to eliminate all bugs from food, the government has guidelines for how many insects and insect fragments are allowed in the food that's sold to the public. An insect fragment might be an antenna, a leg, or a wing.

Inspector Insecto looks at 15 samples of strawberry jam. In each sample, he finds four insect fragments. Each sample has a different combination of antenna, legs, and wings.
List all of the combinations.

What's for Dinner?

Insect fragments in your peanut butter might seem gross, but people around the world eat insects on purpose. They're a good source of protein and low in fat. Silkworms, grasshoppers, and water bugs are sold by the pound in Thailand. In South America, roasted ants are sold in movie theaters instead of popcorn.

Each pizza is topped with a different insect. Unscramble the letters to name the bugs.

hsopgrrepsa   fgdaylnor

kecrcti   retteim

A plexer is a word puzzle that shows a common word or phrase by arranging words in an unusual way. Can you solve these bug-related plexers? The first one is done for you.

YOURantsPANTS : ants in your pants

PANTS
DIRTY

DADDY L E G S

AN AAAAAAAAAA

Congratulations! You've successfully unscrambled these gross brain teasers. Hopefully this is just the beginning of your search for more delightfully disgusting puzzles about yourself and the world around you.

ANSWER KEY

p. 4
DISGUSTING
YUCKY
FOUL
REPULSIVE
REVOLTING
SICKENING
ICKY

p. 5, first problem
5 x 6 = 30, and 8 x 4 = 32 (thirty too).

p. 5, second problem
Move one of the end mites to the opposite end of the row.

p. 6, first problem
18 square feet of skin

p. 6, second problem
about 16,666,667 bacteria (equation: 300 million/18 = 16,666,667)

p. 6, third problem
12,500,000 bacteria

p. 7, first problem
seven towels

p. 7, second problem
Three letter words from BACTERIA (There are more possible answers.)
ATE, ACT, ARE, AIR, ACE, ART, BAT, BET, BIT, BAR, CAR, CAB, CAT, EAR, EAT, ICE, RIB, TEA, TAR, TAB, TIC, RAT, IRE, TIE

p. 8, first problem
MICROSCOPE
TICK
SNEEZE or WHEEZE
SPIDER
POOP
EIGHT

p. 8, second problem
DUST
MUST
MUSE
MUTE
MITE
OR
DUST
MUST
MUTT
MITT
MITE

p. 9, first problem
MOM
DAD
KAYAK
TOOT
NOON

p. 9, second problem
MATTRESS, ARMCHAIR, BLANKETS, CURTAINS

p. 10, first problem
Don't eat food that's been on the floor.

p. 10, second problem
Jennifer wins by 9 points. Her score is 71 and James' is 62.

p. 10, third problem
James cleans for two hours and four minutes, and Jennifer cleans for two hours and 22 minutes.

p. 11, first problem
June 12th

p. 11, second problem
first day: eight barfs
second day: four barfs

p. 12, first problem
On the fourth day

p. 12, second problem
BLOOD
URINE
SWEAT
VOMIT
MUCUS
SALIVA
PUS

p. 13, first problem
SCAB

p. 13, second problem
He's got **ears** on the sides of his head.
They found f**ur in e**very den.
Bra**vo, Mit**chell!

p. 14
EARWAX-MUCUS-SWEAT
SALIVA-BLOOD-TEARS

p. 15, first problem
P
I
C

p. 15, second problem
faces=feces
note=nose
snow=snot
mutt=butt
pure=puke
lives=liver

p. 16
Solution 1: First Sabrina takes the monkey across and leaves it on the other side. She goes back and gets the python, and takes it to the other side. She leaves the python on the other side while she brings the monkey back to the first side. Leaving the monkey,

she takes the bananas across and leaves them. Then she goes back for the monkey. Solution 2: First Sabrina takes the monkey across and leaves it on the other side. She goes back and gets the bananas and takes them to the other side. She leaves the bananas on the other side while she brings the monkey back to the first side. Leaving the monkey, she takes the python across and leaves them. Then she goes back for the monkey.

p. 17

One – just Dave. He sees the caterpillars on his way to the zoo, but nowhere does it say the caterpillars or the people whose shoes were hit with poo are going to the zoo.

p. 18

$3 + (3/3) = 4$

p. 19, first problem

Zoey circles the tree and as Slurpy follows, her rope gets shorter.

p. 19, problem 2

(There may be more correct answers.) spit, slime, saliva, slobber, spittle, sputum

p. 20, first problem

Sam had his paper right-side up, but Sofia accidentally turned her paper upside down and added $1 + 6 + 1 + 6 + 1$

p. 20, second problem

malaria
yellow fever
sleeping sickness
dysentery

p. 21, first problem

a. 81 total flies
equation: $27 \times 3 = 81$ or
$27 + (2 \times 27) = 81$
b. 40.5 inches (102.87 cm)
c. 20.25 inches (51.84 cm)

p. 21, second problem

bacteria, feces, disease, enzymes

p. 22, first problem

Answer #1: First, flip pots 1 and 2. Next, flip pots 1 and 2 again. Third, flip pots 1 and 3.
Answer #2: First, flip pots 2 and 3. Next, flip pots 2 and 3 again. Third, flip pots 1 and 3.

p. 22, second problem

FART
FORT
FOOT
HOOT
HOOP
POOP

p. 23, first problem

Give the fifth soldier his maggot in the dish.

p. 23, second problem

SOLDIERS
WOUNDED
INFECTION
BACTERIA
TISSUE
TREATMENT
DOCTORS

p. 24, first problem

0 0 0 0
0 0 0 0
0 0 0 0
0 0 0 0

p. 24, second problem

SHELL
DOLL
BLOOD
BELCH
SLOB

p. 25, first problem

Bloody
Jumpy
Kooky
Muncher
Slick
Slimy
Tickler
Ugly

p. 25, second problem

Slimy Muncher Slick Kooky Ugly Bloody Tickler Jumpy

p. 26

0 antenna, 1 leg, 3 wings
0 antenna, 2 legs, 2 wings
0 antenna, 3 legs, 1 wing
0 antenna, 0 legs, 4 wings
0 antenna, 4 legs, 0 wings
1 antenna, 0 legs, 3 wings
1 antenna, 1 leg, 2 wings
1 antenna, 2 legs, 1 wing
1 antenna, 3 legs, 0 wings
2 antenna, 0 legs, 2 wings
2 antenna, 1 leg, 1 wing
2 antenna, 2 legs, 0 wings
3 antenna, 0 legs, 1 wing
3 antenna, 1 leg, 0 wings
4 antenna, 0 legs, 0 wings

p. 27, first problem

grasshopper, cricket, dragonfly, termite

p. 27, second problem

ANTS IN YOUR PANTS
DIRTY UNDERPANTS
DADDY LONG LEGS
ANTENNA

Glossary

allergic (uh-LUR-jik)—if you are allergic to something, it causes you to sneeze, develop a rash, or have another unpleasant reaction; people can be allergic to dust, pollen, and foods

bacteria (bak-TEER-ee-uh)—one-celled, microscopic living things that exist all around you and inside you; many bacteria are useful, but some cause disease

decipher (di-SYE-fur)—to figure out something that is written in code or is hard to understand

digest (dy-GEST)—to break down food so it can be used by the body

feces (FEE-seez)—the semi-solid waste that people and animals pass out of their bodies

follicle (FALL-uh-kuhl)—a small sac or cavity in the body, such as for hair

infection (in-FEK-shun)—an illness caused by germs such as bacteria or viruses

microscopic (mye-kruh-SKOP-ik)—too small to be seen without a microscope

phlegm (FLEM)—the thick snot that is produced when someone has a cold

predator (PRED-uh-tur)—an animal that hunts other animals for food

tissue (TISH-yoo)—a layer or bunch of soft material that makes up body parts

urine (YOOR-uhn)—the liquid waste that people and animals pass out of their bodies

Read More

Claybourne, Anna. *100 Most Disgusting Things on the Planet.* New York: Scholastic, 2010.

Leet, Karen M. *Food Intruders: Invisible Creatures Lurking in Your Food.* Tiny Creepy Creatures. North Mankato, Minn.: Capstone Press, 2011.

Miller, Connie Colwell. *This Book Might Make You Gag: A Collection of Crazy, Gross Trivia.* Super Trivia Collection. North Mankato, Minn.: Capstone Press, 2012.

Internet Sites

FactHound offers a safe, fun way to find Internet sites related to this book. All of the sites on FactHound have been researched by our staff.

Here's all you do:

Visit *www.facthound.com*

Type in this code: 9781429699235

 Check out projects, games and lots more at **www.capstonekids.com**

Index